The Best Gift Ever

Shelley Vieira

Illustrated by
Maggui Ledbetter

This book is dedicated to all who ran
a shorter race than hoped and prayed for,
and for those who continue to run with them
forever in their hearts.

"Remember the goodness of God in the FROST of adversity."

–Charles Spurgeon

This book can be sung to the tune
of a childhood favorite, *Frosty the Snowman.*

Jesus my Savior was born to save my soul.
In his strength and might, forever in his sight.
He will help me reach the goal.

The Savior—yes, the Messiah, the Lord has been born today in Bethlehem, the city of David!—Luke 2:11

*Salvation is found in no one else, for there is no other name under heaven
given to mankind by which we must be saved.—Acts 4:1*

I can do all things through him who gives me strength.—Philippians 4:13

*Not that I have already obtained all this, or have already arrived at my goal, but I press on
to take hold of that for which Christ Jesus took hold of me.—Philippians 3:12*

♫♪

Jesus my Savior is no fairytale, I'll say.
For he loves me so, I'm made white as snow,
and he hears me when I pray.

As the Father has loved me, so have I loved you. Abide in my love.—John 15:9

Cleanse me with hyssop, and I will be clean; wash me, and I will be whiter than snow.—Psalm 51:7

Then you will call on me and come and pray to me, and I will listen to you.
You will seek me and find me when you seek me with all your heart.—Jeremiah 29:12-13

♫♪

Faith over fear seems magic.
Trials come yet joy is found.

I sought the Lord, and he answered me; he delivered me from all my fears.—Psalm 34:4

*Consider it pure joy, my brothers and sisters, whenever you face trials of many kinds,
because you know that the testing of your faith produces perseverance. Let perseverance finish its work
so that you may be mature and complete, not lacking anything.—James 1-4*

JOY

♫♪

For when I place my trust in him
I begin to soar around!

*Those who trust in the Lord will renew their strength . They will soar high on wings like eagles.
They will run and not grow weary. They will walk and not faint.—Isaiah 40:31*

*The LORD is my strength and my shield ; my heart trusts in him, and he helps me.
My heart leaps for joy, and with my song I praise him.—Psalm 28:7*

♫♪

Oh, Jesus my Savior is God's gift for you and me! For he came to save and conquered the grave. Bless my heart so I can see.

*Every good and perfect gift is from above, coming down from the Father of the heavenly lights,
who does not change like shifting shadows.—James 1:17*

For the wages of sin is death, but the gift of God is eternal life in Christ Jesus our Lord.—Romans 6:23

*I pray that the eyes of your heart may be enlightened in order that you may know the hope
to which he has called you, the riches of his glorious inheritance in his holy people,
and his incomparably great power for us who believe…—Ephesians 1:18-19*

♫♪

Jesus my savior knew troubles would come my way. So he said, "Run the race. I will give you grace, I am with you always."

I have told you these things, so that in me you may have peace. In this world you will have trouble. But take heart! I have overcome the world.—John 16:33

Let us then approach God's throne of grace with confidence, so that we may receive mercy and find grace to help us in our time of need.— Hebrews 5:16

So do not fear, for I am with you; do not be dismayed, for I am your God. I will strengthen you and help you; I will uphold you with my righteous right hand.—Isaiah 41:10

Down through the valley, a rod and staff in his hand.
Darkness here and there, arrows everywhere!
I sang, "I'm in my Father's hand."

The Lord is my Shepherd, I lack nothing. Even though I walk through the darkest valley, I will fear no evil, for you are with me; your rod and your staff comfort me.—Psalm 23:1,4

You will not fear the terror of night, nor the arrow that flies by day.—Psalm91:5

I give them eternal life, and they shall never perish; no one will snatch them out of my hand.— John 10:28

He placed my feet upon the rock
where I began to see.
The Father knows when sparrows fall,
so he's surely watching me!

*The LORD is the light of my salvation —whom shall I fear. The LORD is the stronghold of my life—
of whom shall I be afraid? For in the day of trouble he will keep me safe in his dwelling;
he will hide me in the shelter of his sacred tent and set me high upon a rock.— Psalm 27:1,5*

Whoever dwells in the shelter of the Most High will rest in the shadow of the Almighty.—Psalm 91:1

*Are not two sparrows sold for a penny? Yet not one of them will fall to the ground outside the Father's care.
So don't be afraid; you are worth more than many sparrows.—Mathew 10:29,31*

♫♪

Jesus my Savior will take me home someday.
Caterpillars crawl, but butterflies fly;
Jesus lives and so will I!

*My Father's house has many rooms; if that were not so, would I have told you that
I am going to prepare a place for you? And If I go and prepare a place for you, I will come back
and take you to be with me that you also may be where I am.—John 14:2-3*

*Before long, the world will not see me anymore, but you will see me.
Because I live , you also will live.—John 14:19*

♫♪

Running-run-run,
Running-run-run,
he will give me grace!

However, I consider my life worth nothing to me; my only aim is to finish the race and complete the task
the Lord Jesus has given me—the task of testifying to the good news of God's grace.—Acts:20:24

But he said to me, "My grace is sufficient for you, for my power is made perfect in weakness. Therefore I will boast
all the more gladly about my weakness, so that Christ's power may rest on me.—2 Corinthians 12:9

♫♪ Running-run-run, Running-run-run, a crown on me he'll place.

Do you not know that in a race all the runners run, but only one gets the prize? Run in such a way as to get the prize. Everyone who competes in the games goes into strict training. They do it to get a crown that will not last, but we do it to get a crown that will last forever.—1 Corinthians 9:24-25

Those the Lord has rescued will return. They will enter Zion with singing; everlasting joy will crown their heads. Gladness and joy will overtake them, and sorrow and sighing will flee away.—Isaiah 51:11

About the Author

Shelley Vieira is a wife, mother, and grandmother (aka Vivi). She Is a resident of both the Central Valley and Central Coast of California. She is the author of *Kingdom Kids*, a book that teaches children to treasure the truth through rhymes and songs, and *Donuts in Love*, a book on the effects of consistent love. Her desire is to lead both young and old to a childlike faith, so they remember how dearly the Father loves and cares for them. She loves to write and purposely places the Living Word of God within the pages she writes. She hopes that the Lord continues to give a sweet tune to accompany all her books because the Lord has been good to her, and therefore, she can't help but sing (Psalm 13:6).

About the Illustrator

Maggui Ledbetter graduated from CSU Fresno with a bachelor's degree and a teaching credential. After teaching for Los Banos Unified School District for thirty years, Maggui retired and now spends her days painting at home in her art studio. She enjoys painting with watercolors and acrylics and has a passion for using art to express the farmer's struggles with water shortages and politics and their love of farming. Maggui has illustrated for books such as *How Far is Heaven*, *Blanket of Miracles*, *Tulip's Journey*, *Donuts in Love*, and her own authored book entitled *The Pink Can Notes*. Maggui looks forward to more years of writing and painting.

If you would like to receive
The Best Gift Ever and
begin a personal relationship with Jesus
today, please pray this prayer:

Lord Jesus, I invite You into my life,
I believe You died for me and that
Your blood pays for my sins and
provides me with the gift of eternal life;
By faith I receive that gift and
thank You for the Holy Spirit
that will now help me in this life.
I accept You as my Lord and Savior.
Amen.